My Heartbeats

your heartbeats our heartbeats

Amitabh Sharma

My Heartbeats

your heartbeats our heartbeats

Amitabh Sharma

PAPER TOWNS
PUBLISHERS

PAPER TOWNS
PUBLISHERS

First published by
Papertowns Publishers
72, Vishwanath Dham Colony,
Niwaru Road, Jhotwara,
Jaipur, 302012

My Heartbeats

ISBN Print Book – 978-93-94670-18-1

Cover by Neha Agrawal
nehaa.2089@gmail.com

Dedicated to all friends,

Your friends, my friends, our friends, who walked the path with us with their hearts full of love.

Acknowledgement

My gratitude to all my friends who walked the path with me, made me feel loved and added to my wisdom & strength throughout my life. A Special thanks to Col. Rakesh Mehra (Retd) for helping me with the theme, and shaping the book.

My sincere thanks to my publishers, Paper Towns, for their creative designs and a hassle-free publication process and Neha for managing my project efficiently.

Last but not the least, gratitude to my parents for everything that I have achieved in life. It wouldn't have been possible without their blessings.

Index

LET LOVE TAKE IT ALL

More than the love
it's the idea of being in love
that keeps us going.
It brings a zeal...makes us heal,
the feel of Love is so surreal,
surrounds us with happiness,
brings joy umpteen.
So let the idea of love afloat and be seen,
Love brings power & is never mean
Let's start at Loving all..
&
Let love take it all..!!"

I DON’T MISS YOU

I don't miss you, my friend,
Not because you don't love and care anymore,
Not because you are with someone else,
Not because you don't communicate,
Not because you misjudged me,
Not because you called me names,
I don't miss you...
because
I know you are happy where you are,
Far and away, but always in my heart.
I don't miss you, my friend, because you are
always in my heart...

WHAT IF I STOP TALKING TO YOU

I would talk to you nonetheless,
Talk to you in imagination,
Talk to you in dreams,
Talk to you through letters,
Talk to you through friends,
My talks will never end, my friend,
Until your deafening silence ends...

YOU, MY SELF-LOVE

Why do you love me?

Because...

Loving you is like loving me...!!

MY GIFTS FOR HER

She was richly beautiful,
logical and sound.
Wondered what gift
would make her profound.
Pondered and found,
She missed the twinkle in her eyes
And usual chuckle in her sound.
Too expensive to be found.
Wish I could buy a smile for her face
and
giggle for her sound.

LOVE IS NOT A DECLARATION

Love you, is an exclamation,
Love you, friend, is an expression.
What's love without expressions?
Love is not a declaration."

You.
Me.

AS THINGS BE FINE-'YOU & ME'

Things will be fine again,
You will be you & I will be me again.
You will immerse in ambition and dreams,
I will be back to earning beans.
The rat race will begin again.
Wonder if we'll ever have time again.
Let's live this moment.
Never know if we will ever meet again.
'You'll be you and I'll be Me' again.
Wonder if we will ever be US again...!!

A DIFFERENT LOVE STORY

He was married, yet single.
She was single, but married to the past.
Both were different, yet became friends quite fast.
Together, they began to plan their future,
But social stigmas didn't let it go far.
She walked out of the friendship
And chose a new path.
She got married and turned single.
He turned single and married the past.

PROPOSALS

Proposals must be rehearsed, guys,
Because when the time comes,
One is always at a loss of words...!!

RELATIONSHIPS

Head over heels is painful infatuation,
Being in love is a feeling.
In a relationship is a status.
Marriage is a certain certificate.
Friendship is
the only genuine relationship

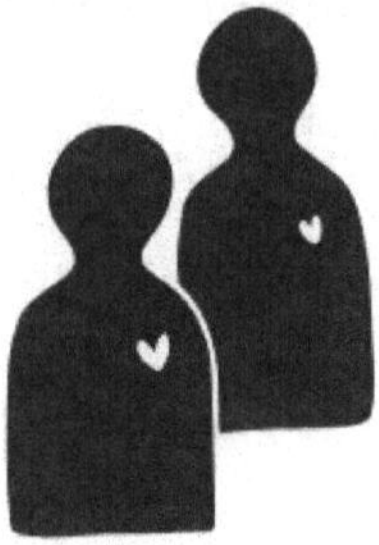

DEFINING LOVE

Love is
all about being fond of,
Not just being involved.
Involvement in relationship happens,
Fondness doesn't.
Fondness just pours love.

TÊTE-À-TÊTE WITH MISTAKES

Lying alone in my room,
Aloof in my heart space,
I wondered if my mistakes could speak.
Where did I err?
How did I go wrong?
As an epiphany, the mistake appeared and said,
You told the truth and broke a heart.
Now the good in you woos the broken heart.
The heart which is hurt, now hurts you too.

MUSTN'T A MAN ALWAYS STAY BRIGHT?

She wanted to go and he hardly had a choice,
But she also needed to feel justified.
So, she blamed him outright.
His closeness to a friend not deemed right
Not wanting to hide feelings and also to hold friends' pride.
He shared his pain with the friend, being uptight.
In shock and awe, she too, decided to go
Again, he had no choice
But she, too, wanted to feel justified,
She, too, blamed him of severing ties.
Wonder if anyone worried about his plight.
Mustn't a man always stay bright...!!

SOMETIMES

Sometimes love is
Impatient and unkind,
It envies and boasts of mine,
It germinates doubts and obsessions,
Blurs love and infatuation.
Turns compassion into passion
and
Leaves a lot of life lessons.

MY HEART

It takes a lot of beating,

still...

helps me follow my life's path.

ENERGETICALLY TIED

He let her go because she felt tied,
She happily took a flight
to distant heights
far and away to her delight.
The journey was bright
but she had no respite,
her mind was free but the heart cried.
Something remained amiss,
Though freed, she was,
but energetically tied.

LOVE HARASSMENTS

If true love is harassment,
I wish and request you, my friend,
Please harass me forever.

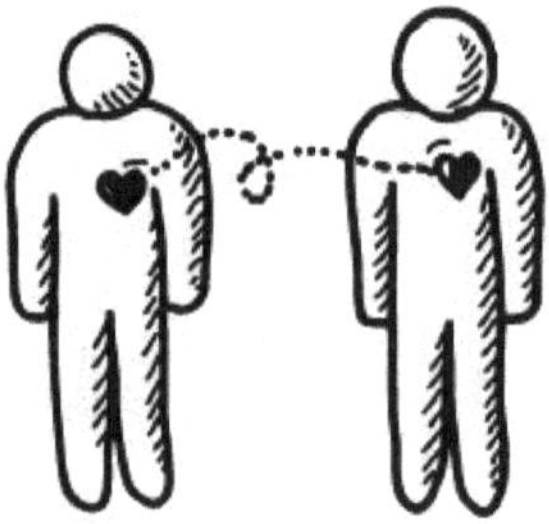

LOVE FOR NO REASON

Don't know why
I miss her more than others.
Don’t know why
feel goosebumps by her attention.
Don’t know why
feel overly happy in her presence.
Don’t know why
always miss her absence
Don't know why
I love her without reason
Guess some connections
have no explanations.

LOVE AND FRIENDSHIP

Friendship is the most
misunderstood thing today.
If you say ‘I love you’ to your friend,
then the friend unfriends you.
If you say ‘I don't’, you are followed
If you say you fascinate me, you are adored.
If you say you are loved, you are abhorred.

WHEN IS IT LOVE?

Do you know when it is love?
It's when the eyes meet,
the heart throbs,
the smiles exchange,
and yet we wonder,
'Is it love?'

NO CONTACT

What's it when
a friend unfriends you,
Deletes your comments,
and blocks you
on all social media.
Is it pain, angst, hatefulness?
Whatever...
Wish it has some love, too.

ILLUSION OF LOVE

I realised...

It was the illusion...of love..

Illusion of her being the perfect one...

Illusion of her bringing the best out of me...

Illusion of her being my best ever pal......

Illusion of me not being me without her....

Illusions were mine...n...mine alone..

Illusions were mine of love...

BLESSED BY LOVE

You are blessed if you are loved by someone
Blessed if desired,
Blessed if cared,
Blessed if longed for and awaited,
Blessed if respected
and
blessed truly indeed for life....
if befriended by someone, who embraces it all

THE CONNECT

I had hardly known her

but...

the connect made it difficult to believe

that

I had hardly known her...

LOVE NEVER FALLS... NEVER FAILS

Easy to fall and easy to fail,
Difficult to find and even difficult to retain,
never say 'better luck next time'
And never say 'never again'
Rise and Shine in love,
As in love
one never falls and never ever fails.

B
F

FRIENDS HURT

Why do we misunderstand friends?
Why do we misunderstand love & care?
Why do we call names to friends?
&
Why do we make them 'Once friends'?
Why do we keep away, though near?
Why do we remain apart, though close?
Why do we talk in dreams and not in reality?
Why do we misunderstand friends?
Why do we hurt friends?

TRUE FRIENDS

Friends who miss you
in your absence
are the true friends.

WHY LOVE WALKS AWAY

People leave
for the fear of commitment,
Unsure of self-worth
Desirous to explore more
And many a times
In denial of love.

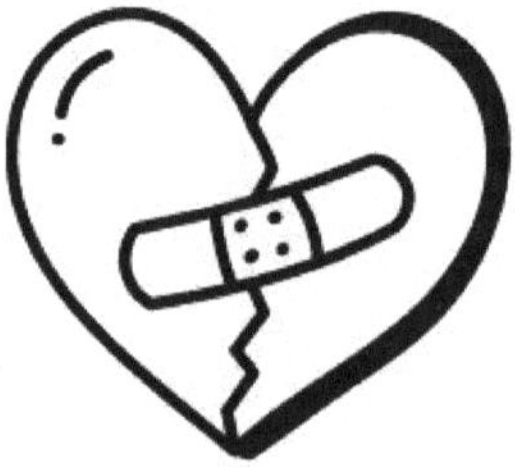

THE MORE I DESIRED, THE MORE I LOST

The more I started to understand her,
The more she started to misunderstand.
The more I started to connect,
The more she started to disconnect.
The more I started to love,
The more she started to detest.
The more I desired,
The more I lost.

TRUST A FRIEND

When you hear 'I love you',
Trust...
When you hear 'I love you, friend',
Trust more...
because
In a mere 'I love you'
You may not have love,
nor
a friend... either..!!

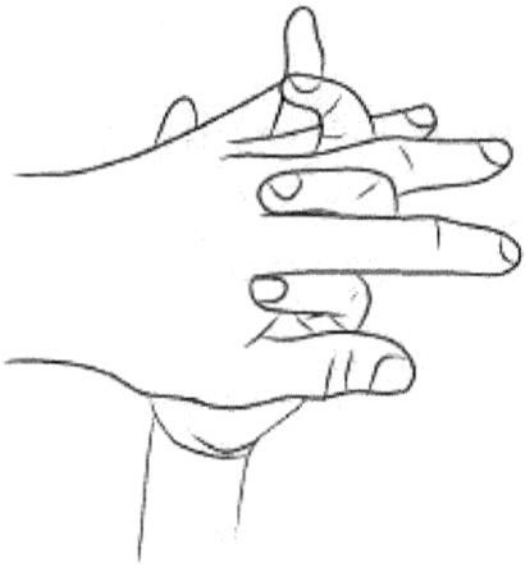

LOVE HAPPENS, FRIENDS DON’T

Love happens anyways,

but friends don't.

Treat them as treasure.

Keep them close.

Friends don’t happen often anymore...!!